VIOLA

101 MOVIE HITS

Available for
FLUTE, CLARINET, ALTO SAX, TENOR SAX, TRUMPET,
HORN, TROMBONE, VIOLIN, VIOLA, CELLO

ISBN 978-1-4950-6071-7

7777 W. BLUEMOUND RD. P.O. BOX 13819 MILWAUKEE, WI 53213

Visit Hal Leonard Online at
www.halleonard.com

CONTENTS

4   Against All Odds (Take a Look at Me Now)

5   Alfie

6   Axel F

7   Baby Elephant Walk

8   Beauty and the Beast

9   Blaze of Glory

10   Blue Velvet

11   Born Free

12   Call Me

14   Can You Feel the Love Tonight

15   Can't Help Falling in Love

16   The Candy Man

17   Chariots of Fire

18   Colors of the Wind

20   Come Saturday Morning

22   Come What May

21   Cups (When I'm Gone)

24   Danger Zone

25   Dear Heart

26   Diamonds Are a Girl's Best Friend

27   Do You Know Where You're Going To?

28   Don't You (Forget About Me)

29   The Dreame

30   End of the Road

31   Endless Love

32   Everybody's Talkin' (Echoes)

33   Exhale (Shoop Shoop)

34   Eye of the Tiger

35   Footloose

36   Forrest Gump - Main Title (Feather Theme)

38   Glory of Love

37   Hallelujah

40   Happy

41   The Heat Is On

42   Hello Again

43   How Deep Is Your Love

44   I Am a Man of Constant Sorrow

45   I Believe I Can Fly

46   I Just Called to Say I Love You

47   I Will Always Love You

48   I Will Wait for You

49   (I've Had) The Time of My Life

50   Jailhouse Rock

51   The John Dunbar Theme

52   Kokomo

54   Let It Go

53   Let the River Run

56   Live and Let Die

57   The Look of Love

58   Luck Be a Lady

59   A Man and a Woman (Un homme et une femme)

60   Maniac

61   Mission: Impossible Theme

62   Mrs. Robinson

63   Moon River

64   More (Ti guarderò nel cuore)

65   The Music of Goodbye

66   My Heart Will Go On (Love Theme from 'Titanic')

67   Nine to Five

68   Nothing's Gonna Stop Us Now

70   Old Time Rock & Roll

71   The Pink Panther

72   Put Your Dreams Away (For Another Day)

73   Puttin' On the Ritz

74   Que Sera, Sera (Whatever Will Be, Will Be)

75   The Rainbow Connection

76   Raindrops Keep Fallin' on My Head

77   Rock Around the Clock

78   Love Theme from "St. Elmo's Fire"

79   Say You, Say Me

80   Separate Lives

82   The Shadow of Your Smile

84   Skyfall

83   Somewhere in Time

86   Somewhere, My Love

87   Somewhere Out There

88   The Sound of Music

89   Speak Softly, Love

90   Star Trek® The Motion Picture

92   Stayin' Alive

91   Summer Nights

94   The Sweetheart Tree

95   Swinging on a Star

96   Take My Breath Away

98   Tammy

99   Thanks for the Memory

100   That's Amoré (That's Love)

101   A Time for Us

102   Time Warp

104   To Sir, With Love

106   Two Hearts

105   Unchained Melody

108   Up Where We Belong

109   The Way We Were

110   When She Loved Me

112   When You Believe

113   When You Wish Upon a Star

114   Where Do I Begin

115   Writing's on the Wall

116   You Light Up My Life

117   You Must Love Me

AGAINST ALL ODDS
(Take a Look at Me Now)
from AGAINST ALL ODDS

VIOLA

Words and Music by
PHIL COLLINS

ALFIE
Theme from the Paramount Picture ALFIE

VIOLA

Words by HAL DAVID
Music by BURT BACHARACH

Slowly, freely

AXEL F
Theme from the Paramount Motion Picture BEVERLY HILLS COP

VIOLA

By HAROLD FALTERMEYER

BABY ELEPHANT WALK
from the Paramount Picture HATARI!

VIOLA

By HENRY MANCINI

BEAUTY AND THE BEAST

from Walt Disney's BEAUTY AND THE BEAST

VIOLA

Music by ALAN MENKEN
Lyrics by HOWARD ASHMAN

BLAZE OF GLORY

featured in the film YOUNG GUNS II

VIOLA

Words and Music by
JON BON JOVI

Moderately slow Rock

1.

2.

D.S. al Fine
(take 2nd ending)

Fine

BLUE VELVET
featured in the Motion Picture BLUE VELVET

VIOLA

Words and Music by BERNIE WAYNE
and LEE MORRIS

BORN FREE

from the Columbia Pictures' Release BORN FREE

VIOLA

Words by DON BLACK
Music by JOHN BARRY

CALL ME
from the Paramount Motion Picture AMERICAN GIGOLO

VIOLA

Words by DEBORAH HARRY
Music by GIORGIO MORODER

CAN YOU FEEL THE LOVE TONIGHT
from Walt Disney Pictures' THE LION KING

VIOLA

Music by ELTON JOHN
Lyrics by TIM RICE

Pop Ballad

CAN'T HELP FALLING IN LOVE

from the Paramount Picture BLUE HAWAII

VIOLA

Words and Music by GEORGE DAVID WEISS,
HUGO PERETTI and LUIGI CREATORE

THE CANDY MAN

from WILLY WONKA AND THE CHOCOLATE FACTORY

VIOLA

Words and Music by LESLIE BRICUSSE
and ANTHONY NEWLEY

CHARIOTS OF FIRE
from CHARIOTS OF FIRE

VIOLA

By VANGELIS

COLORS OF THE WIND

from Walt Disney's POCAHONTAS

VIOLA

Music by ALAN MENKEN
Lyrics by STEPHEN SCHWARTZ

Moderately

To Coda

D.S. al Coda

CODA

COME SATURDAY MORNING
(Saturday Morning)
from the Paramount Picture THE STERILE CUCKOO

VIOLA

Words by DORY PREVIN
Music by FRED KARLIN

Slowly, in 1

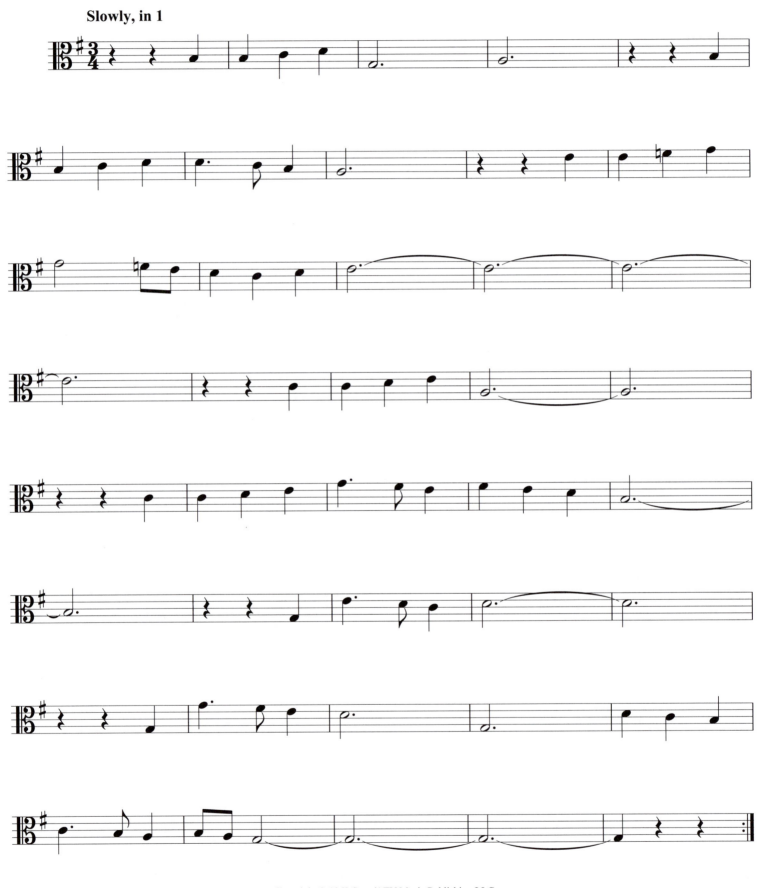

CUPS
(When I'm Gone)
from the Motion Picture Soundtrack PITCH PERFECT

VIOLA

Words and Music by A.P. CARTER,
LUISA GERSTEIN and HELOISE TUNSTALL-BEHRENS

COME WHAT MAY
from the Motion Picture MOULIN ROUGE

VIOLA

Words and Music by
DAVID BAERWALD

DANGER ZONE

from the Motion Picture TOP GUN

VIOLA

Words and Music by GIORGIO MORODER
and TOM WHITLOCK

DEAR HEART
from DEAR HEART

VIOLA

Music by HENRY MANCINI
Words by JAY LIVINGSTON and RAY EVANS

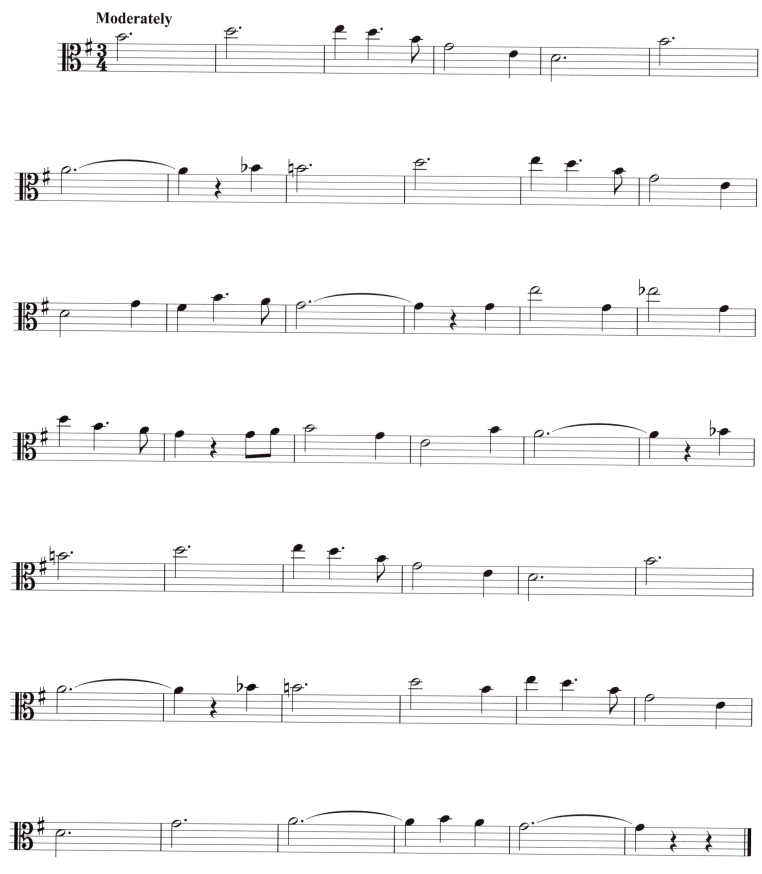

DIAMONDS ARE A GIRL'S BEST FRIEND

from GENTLEMEN PREFER BLONDES

VIOLA

Words by LEO ROBIN
Music by JULE STYNE

DO YOU KNOW WHERE YOU'RE GOING TO?

Theme from MAHOGANY

VIOLA

Words by GERRY GOFFIN
Music by MICHAEL MASSER

DON'T YOU (FORGET ABOUT ME)

from the Universal Picture THE BREAKFAST CLUB

Words and Music by KEITH FORSEY
and STEVE SCHIFF

THE DREAME
from the film SENSE AND SENSIBILITY

VIOLA

By PATRICK DOYLE

Moderately slow

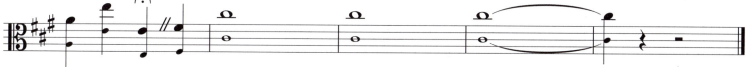

END OF THE ROAD

from the Paramount Motion Picture BOOMERANG

VIOLA

Words and Music by BABYFACE,
L.A. REID and DARYL SIMMONS

ENDLESS LOVE

from ENDLESS LOVE

VIOLA

Words and Music by
LIONEL RICHIE

Moderately slow

EVERYBODY'S TALKIN'

(Echoes)

from MIDNIGHT COWBOY

Words and Music by
FRED NEIL

VIOLA

EXHALE
(Shoop Shoop)
from WAITING TO EXHALE

VIOLA

Words and Music by
BABYFACE

EYE OF THE TIGER
Theme from ROCKY III

VIOLA

Words and Music by FRANK SULLIVAN
and JIM PETERIK

FOOTLOOSE
Theme from the Paramount Motion Picture FOOTLOOSE

VIOLA

Words by DEAN PITCHFORD
Music by KENNY LOGGINS

FORREST GUMP – MAIN TITLE
(Feather Theme)

from the Paramount Motion Picture FORREST GUMP

VIOLA

Music by ALAN SILVESTRI

HALLELUJAH

featured in the DreamWorks Motion Picture SHREK

VIOLA

Words and Music by
LEONARD COHEN

Moderately slow, in 2

GLORY OF LOVE
Theme from KARATE KID PART II

VIOLA

Words and Music by DAVID FOSTER,
PETER CETERA and DIANE NINI

Slowly

HAPPY
from DESPICABLE ME 2

Words and Music by
PHARRELL WILLIAMS

VIOLA

Moderately fast

THE HEAT IS ON
from the Paramount Motion Picture BEVERLY HILLS COP

VIOLA

Words by KEITH FORSEY
Music by HAROLD FALTERMEYER

Moderately fast Rock

HELLO AGAIN

from the Motion Picture THE JAZZ SINGER

VIOLA

Words by NEIL DIAMOND
Music by NEIL DIAMOND
and ALAN LINDGREN

HOW DEEP IS YOUR LOVE
from the Motion Picture SATURDAY NIGHT FEVER

VIOLA

Words and Music by BARRY GIBB,
ROBIN GIBB and MAURICE GIBB

I AM A MAN OF CONSTANT SORROW

featured in O BROTHER, WHERE ART THOU?

VIOLA

Words and Music by
CARTER STANLEY

I BELIEVE I CAN FLY

from SPACE JAM

VIOLA

Words and Music by
ROBERT KELLY

I JUST CALLED TO SAY I LOVE YOU

featured in THE WOMAN IN RED

VIOLA

Words and Music by
STEVIE WONDER

I WILL ALWAYS LOVE YOU

featured in THE BODYGUARD

VIOLA

Words and Music by
DOLLY PARTON

Moderately slow

small notes optional

48

I WILL WAIT FOR YOU
from THE UMBRELLAS OF CHERBOURG

VIOLA

Music by MICHEL LEGRAND
Original French Text by JACQUES DEMY
English Words by NORMAN GIMBEL

(I'VE HAD) THE TIME OF MY LIFE

from DIRTY DANCING

VIOLA

Words and Music by FRANKE PREVITE,
JOHN DeNICOLA and DONALD MARKOWITZ

JAILHOUSE ROCK
from JAILHOUSE ROCK

VIOLA

Words and Music by JERRY LEIBER
and MIKE STOLLER

THE JOHN DUNBAR THEME
from DANCES WITH WOLVES

VIOLA

By JOHN BARRY

Moderately

KOKOMO
from the Motion Picture COCKTAIL

VIOLA

Words and Music by JOHN PHILLIPS,
TERRY MELCHER, MIKE LOVE,
and SCOTT McKENZIE

Moderately bright

LET THE RIVER RUN
Theme from the Motion Picture WORKING GIRL

VIOLA

Words and Music by
CARLY SIMON

LET IT GO
from Disney's Animated Feature FROZEN

VIOLA

Music and Lyrics by KRISTEN ANDERSON-LOPEZ
and ROBERT LOPEZ

Slowly, in 2

Fine

D.S. al Fine

LIVE AND LET DIE

from LIVE AND LET DIE

VIOLA

Words and Music by PAUL McCARTNEY
and LINDA McCARTNEY

THE LOOK OF LOVE

from CASINO ROYALE

VIOLA

Words by HAL DAVID
Music by BURT BACHARACH

Moderately

LUCK BE A LADY

from GUYS AND DOLLS

VIOLA

By FRANK LOESSER

A MAN AND A WOMAN
(Un homme et une femme)
from A MAN AND A WOMAN

VIOLA

Original Words by PIERRE BAROUH
English Words by JERRY KELLER
Music by FRANCIS LAI

MANIAC

from the Paramount Picture FLASHDANCE

VIOLA

Words and Music by MICHAEL SEMBELLO
and DENNIS MATKOSKY

MISSION: IMPOSSIBLE THEME

from the Paramount Motion Picture MISSION: IMPOSSIBLE

VIOLA

By LALO SCHIFRIN

MRS. ROBINSON

from THE GRADUATE

VIOLA

Words and Music by
PAUL SIMON

MOON RIVER

from the Paramount Picture BREAKFAST AT TIFFANY'S

VIOLA

Words by JOHNNY MERCER
Music by HENRY MANCINI

Slowly

MORE
(Ti guarderò nel cuore)
from the film MONDO CANE

VIOLA

Music by NINO OLIVIERO and RIZ ORTOLANI
Italian Lyrics by MARCELLO CIORCIOLINI
English Lyrics by NORMAN NEWELL

THE MUSIC OF GOODBYE

from OUT OF AFRICA

VIOLA

Words and Music by JOHN BARRY,
ALAN BERGMAN and MARILYN BERGMAN

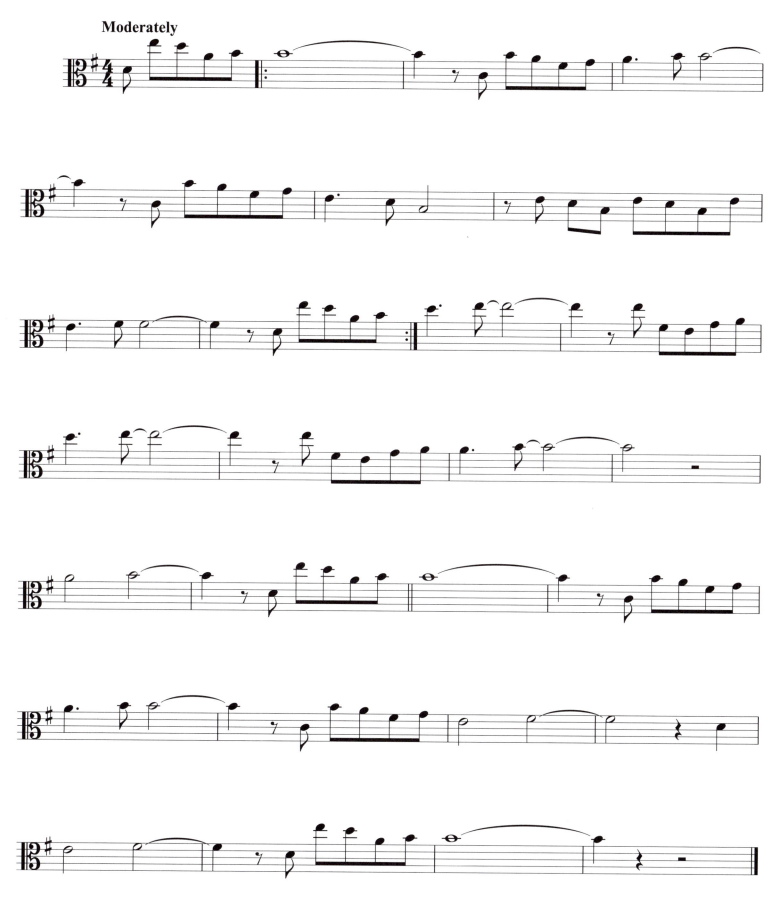

MY HEART WILL GO ON
(Love Theme from 'Titanic')
from the Paramount and Twentieth Century Fox Motion Picture TITANIC

VIOLA

Music by JAMES HORNER
Lyric by WILL JENNINGS

NINE TO FIVE

from NINE TO FIVE

VIOLA

Words and Music by
DOLLY PARTON

Moderately, in 2

D.C. al Coda
(take repeat)

CODA

NOTHING'S GONNA STOP US NOW

featured in MANNEQUIN

VIOLA

Words and Music by DIANE WARREN
and ALBERT HAMMOND

OLD TIME ROCK & ROLL

featured in RISKY BUSINESS

VIOLA

Words and Music by GEORGE JACKSON
and THOMAS E. JONES III

THE PINK PANTHER
from THE PINK PANTHER

VIOLA

By HENRY MANCINI

Moderately, in 4

PUT YOUR DREAMS AWAY (FOR ANOTHER DAY)

featured in INSIDE MOVES

VIOLA

Words by RUTH LOWE
Music by STEPHAN WEISS
and PAUL MANN

PUTTIN' ON THE RITZ

from the Motion Picture PUTTIN' ON THE RITZ

VIOLA

Words and Music by
IRVING BERLIN

Moderately, in 2

QUE SERA, SERA
(Whatever Will Be, Will Be)
from THE MAN WHO KNEW TOO MUCH

VIOLA

Words and Music by JAY LIVINGSTON
and RAYMOND B. EVANS

THE RAINBOW CONNECTION
from THE MUPPET MOVIE

VIOLA

Words and Music by PAUL WILLIAMS
and KENNETH L. ASCHER

Flowing Waltz tempo

RAINDROPS KEEP FALLIN' ON MY HEAD

from BUTCH CASSIDY AND THE SUNDANCE KID

Lyrics by HAL DAVID
Music by BURT BACHARACH

ROCK AROUND THE CLOCK

featured in the Motion Picture BLACKBOARD JUNGLE

Words and Music by MAX C. FREEDMAN
and JIMMY DeKNIGHT

VIOLA

LOVE THEME FROM "ST. ELMO'S FIRE"

from the Motion Picture ST. ELMO'S FIRE

VIOLA

Words and Music by
DAVID FOSTER

SAY YOU, SAY ME

from the Motion Picture WHITE NIGHTS

VIOLA

Words and Music by
LIONEL RICHIE

SEPARATE LIVES
Love Theme from WHITE NIGHTS

VIOLA

Words and Music by
STEPHEN BISHOP

Freely

THE SHADOW OF YOUR SMILE
Love Theme from THE SANDPIPER

VIOLA

Music by JOHNNY MANDEL
Words by PAUL FRANCIS WEBSTER

Slowly, in 2

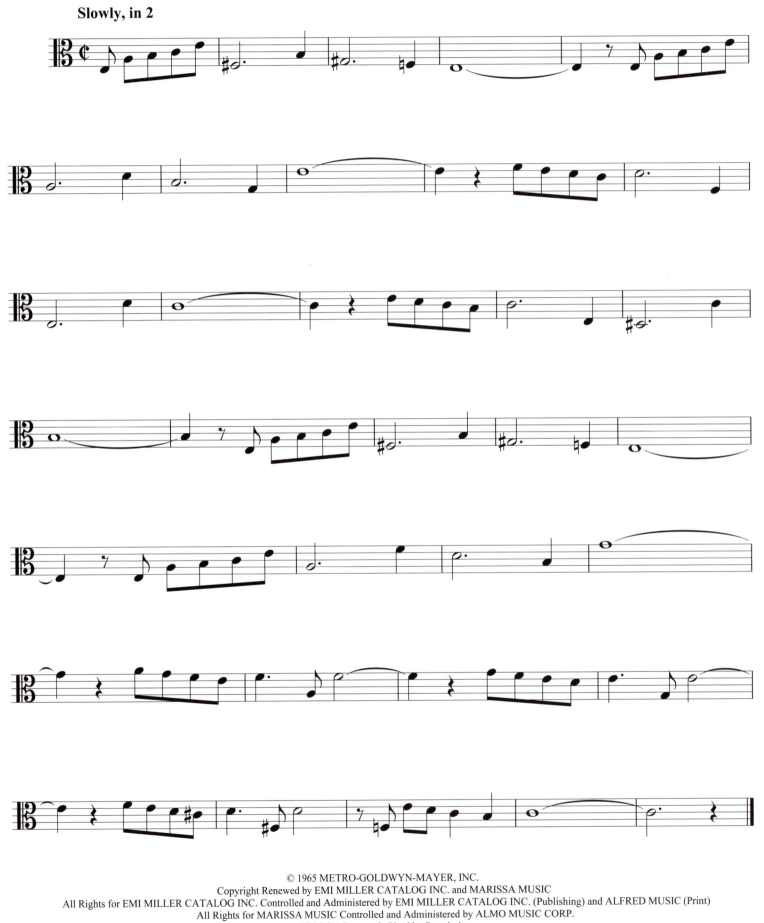

SOMEWHERE IN TIME
from SOMEWHERE IN TIME

VIOLA

By JOHN BARRY

SKYFALL
from the Motion Picture SKYFALL

VIOLA

Words and Music by ADELE ADKINS
and PAUL EPWORTH

SOMEWHERE, MY LOVE

Lara's Theme from DOCTOR ZHIVAGO

VIOLA

Lyric by PAUL FRANCIS WEBSTER
Music by MAURICE JARRE

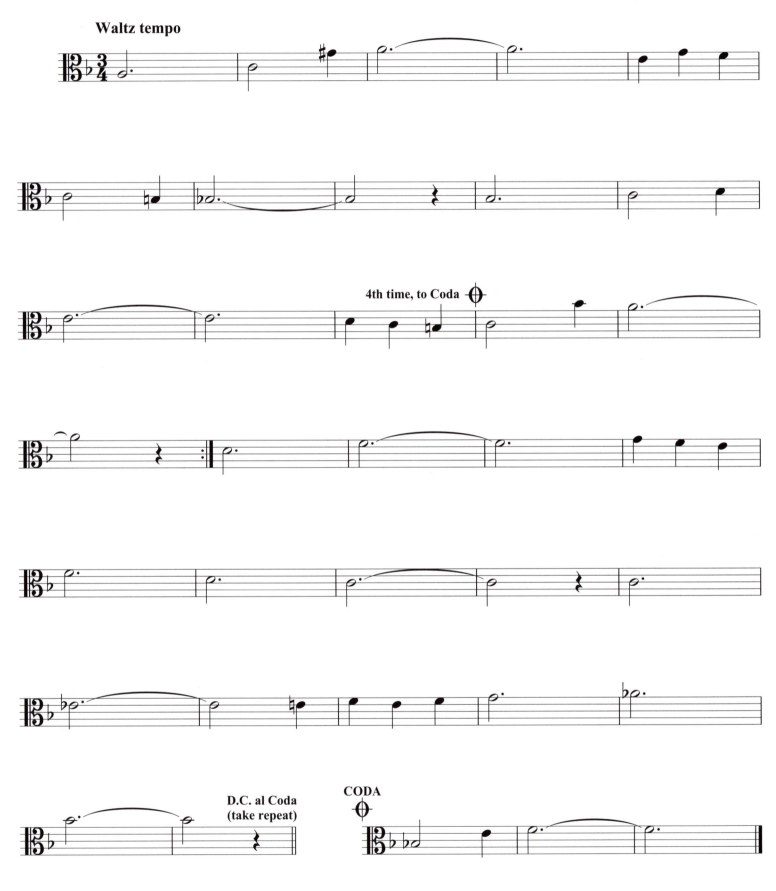

Somewhere Out There

from AN AMERICAN TAIL

VIOLA

Music by BARRY MANN and JAMES HORNER
Lyrics by CYNTHIA WEIL

THE SOUND OF MUSIC

from THE SOUND OF MUSIC

VIOLA

Lyrics by OSCAR HAMMERSTEIN II
Music by RICHARD RODGERS

SPEAK SOFTLY, LOVE
(Love Theme)
from the Paramount Picture THE GODFATHER

VIOLA

Words by LARRY KUSIK
Music by NINO ROTA

STAR TREK® THE MOTION PICTURE

Theme from the Paramount Picture STAR TREK: THE MOTION PICTURE

VIOLA

Music by
JERRY GOLDSMITH

SUMMER NIGHTS

from GREASE

VIOLA

Lyric and Music by WARREN CASEY
and JIM JACOBS

STAYIN' ALIVE
from the Motion Picture SATURDAY NIGHT FEVER

VIOLA

Words and Music by BARRY GIBB,
ROBIN GIBB and MAURICE GIBB

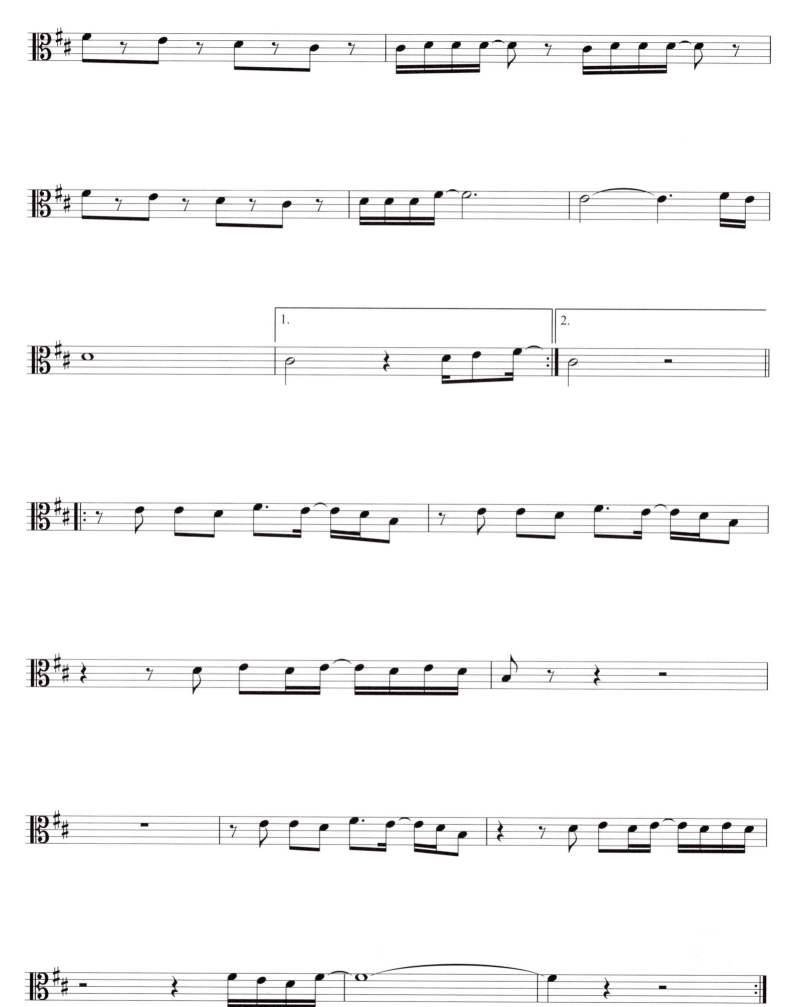

THE SWEETHEART TREE

from THE GREAT RACE

VIOLA

Words by JOHNNY MERCER
Music by HENRY MANCINI

SWINGING ON A STAR

from GOING MY WAY

VIOLA

Words by JOHNNY BURKE
Music by JIMMY VAN HEUSEN

TAKE MY BREATH AWAY
(Love Theme)
from the Paramount Picture TOP GUN

VIOLA

Words and Music by GIORGIO MORODER
and TOM WHITLOCK

TAMMY
from TAMMY AND THE BACHELOR

VIOLA

Words and Music by JAY LIVINGSTON
and RAY EVANS

THANKS FOR THE MEMORY

from the Paramount Picture BIG BROADCAST OF 1938

VIOLA

Words and Music by LEO ROBIN
and RALPH RAINGER

THAT'S AMORÉ
(That's Love)
from the Paramount Picture THE CADDY

VIOLA

Words by JACK BROOKS
Music by HARRY WARREN

A TIME FOR US
(Love Theme)
from the Paramount Picture ROMEO AND JULIET

VIOLA

Words by LARRY KUSIK
and EDDIE SNYDER
Music by NINO ROTA

Moderately slow

TIME WARP
from THE ROCKY HORROR PICTURE SHOW

Words and Music by
RICHARD O'BRIEN

VIOLA

Moderately fast Rock

TO SIR, WITH LOVE

from TO SIR, WITH LOVE

VIOLA

Words by DON BLACK
Music by MARC LONDON

UNCHAINED MELODY

from the Motion Picture UNCHAINED

VIOLA

Lyric by HY ZARET
Music by ALEX NORTH

TWO HEARTS

from BUSTER

VIOLA

Words and Music by PHIL COLLINS
and LAMONT DOZIER

UP WHERE WE BELONG

from the Paramount Picture AN OFFICER AND A GENTLEMAN

Words by WILL JENNINGS
Music by BUFFY SAINTE-MARIE and JACK NITZSCHE

VIOLA

THE WAY WE WERE

from the Motion Picture THE WAY WE WERE

VIOLA

Words by ALAN and MARILYN BERGMAN
Music by MARVIN HAMLISCH

WHEN SHE LOVED ME

from Walt Disney Pictures' TOY STORY 2 - A Pixar Film

VIOLA

Music and Lyrics by
RANDY NEWMAN

Slowly and freely

WHEN YOU BELIEVE
(From The Prince of Egypt)
from THE PRINCE OF EGYPT

VIOLA

Words and Music by
STEPHEN SCHWARTZ

WHEN YOU WISH UPON A STAR

from Walt Disney's PINOCCHIO

VIOLA

Words by NED WASHINGTON
Music by LEIGH HARLINE

WHERE DO I BEGIN

(Love Theme)

from the Paramount Picture LOVE STORY

VIOLA

Words by CARL SIGMAN
Music by FRANCIS LAI

WRITING'S ON THE WALL

from the film SPECTRE

VIOLA

Words and Music by SAM SMITH
and JAMES NAPIER

Slowly

YOU LIGHT UP MY LIFE

from YOU LIGHT UP MY LIFE

VIOLA

Words and Music by
JOSEPH BROOKS

YOU MUST LOVE ME

from the Cinergi Motion Picture EVITA

VIOLA

Words by TIM RICE
Music by ANDREW LLOYD WEBBER

101 SONGS

BIG COLLECTIONS OF FAVORITE SONGS ARRANGED FOR SOLO INSTRUMENTALISTS.

101 BROADWAY SONGS

00154199	Flute	$15.99
00154200	Clarinet	$15.99
00154201	Alto Sax	$15.99
00154202	Tenor Sax	$16.99
00154203	Trumpet	$15.99
00154204	Horn	$15.99
00154205	Trombone	$15.99
00154206	Violin	$15.99
00154207	Viola	$15.99
00154208	Cello	$15.99

101 DISNEY SONGS

00244104	Flute	$17.99
00244106	Clarinet	$17.99
00244107	Alto Sax	$17.99
00244108	Tenor Sax	$17.99
00244109	Trumpet	$17.99
00244112	Horn	$17.99
00244120	Trombone	$17.99
00244121	Violin	$17.99
00244125	Viola	$17.99
00244126	Cello	$17.99

101 MOVIE HITS

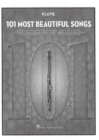

00158087	Flute	$15.99
00158088	Clarinet	$15.99
00158089	Alto Sax	$15.99
00158090	Tenor Sax	$15.99
00158091	Trumpet	$15.99
00158092	Horn	$15.99
00158093	Trombone	$15.99
00158094	Violin	$15.99
00158095	Viola	$15.99
00158096	Cello	$15.99

101 CHRISTMAS SONGS

00278637	Flute	$15.99
00278638	Clarinet	$15.99
00278639	Alto Sax	$15.99
00278640	Tenor Sax	$15.99
00278641	Trumpet	$15.99
00278642	Horn	$14.99
00278643	Trombone	$15.99
00278644	Violin	$15.99
00278645	Viola	$15.99
00278646	Cello	$15.99

101 HIT SONGS

00194561	Flute	$17.99
00197182	Clarinet	$17.99
00197183	Alto Sax	$17.99
00197184	Tenor Sax	$17.99
00197185	Trumpet	$17.99
00197186	Horn	$17.99
00197187	Trombone	$17.99
00197188	Violin	$17.99
00197189	Viola	$17.99
00197190	Cello	$17.99

101 POPULAR SONGS

00224722	Flute	$17.99
00224723	Clarinet	$17.99
00224724	Alto Sax	$17.99
00224725	Tenor Sax	$17.99
00224726	Trumpet	$17.99
00224727	Horn	$17.99
00224728	Trombone	$17.99
00224729	Violin	$17.99
00224730	Viola	$17.99
00224731	Cello	$17.99

101 CLASSICAL THEMES

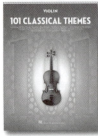

00155315	Flute	$15.99
00155317	Clarinet	$15.99
00155318	Alto Sax	$15.99
00155319	Tenor Sax	$15.99
00155320	Trumpet	$15.99
00155321	Horn	$15.99
00155322	Trombone	$15.99
00155323	Violin	$15.99
00155324	Viola	$15.99
00155325	Cello	$15.99

101 JAZZ SONGS

00146363	Flute	$15.99
00146364	Clarinet	$15.99
00146366	Alto Sax	$15.99
00146367	Tenor Sax	$15.99
00146368	Trumpet	$15.99
00146369	Horn	$14.99
00146370	Trombone	$15.99
00146371	Violin	$15.99
00146372	Viola	$15.99
00146373	Cello	$15.99

101 MOST BEAUTIFUL SONGS

00291023	Flute	$16.99
00291041	Clarinet	$16.99
00291042	Alto Sax	$17.99
00291043	Tenor Sax	$17.99
00291044	Trumpet	$16.99
00291045	Horn	$16.99
00291046	Trombone	$16.99
00291047	Violin	$16.99
00291048	Viola	$16.99
00291049	Cello	$17.99

See complete song lists and sample pages at www.halleonard.com

HAL•LEONARD®
www.halleonard.com

0222

The Best-Selling Jazz Book of All Time Is Now Legal!

The Real Books are the most popular jazz books of all time. Since the 1970s, musicians have trusted these volumes to get them through every gig, night after night. The problem is that the books were illegally produced and distributed, without any regard to copyright law, or royalties paid to the composers who created these musical masterpieces.

Hal Leonard is very proud to present the first legitimate and legal editions of these books ever produced. You won't even notice the difference, other than all the notorious errors being fixed: the covers and typeface look the same, the song lists are nearly identical, and the price for our edition is even cheaper than the originals!

Every conscientious musician will appreciate that these books are now produced accurately and ethically, benefitting the songwriters that we owe for some of the greatest tunes of all time!

VOLUME 1
00240221	C Edition	$39.99
00240224	B♭ Edition	$39.99
00240225	E♭ Edition	$39.99
00240226	Bass Clef Edition	$39.99
00286389	F Edition	$39.99
00240292	C Edition 6 x 9	$35.00
00240339	B♭ Edition 6 x 9	$35.00
00147792	Bass Clef Edition 6 x 9	$35.00
00451087	C Edition on CD-ROM	$29.99
00200984	Online Backing Tracks: Selections	$45.00
00110604	Book/USB Flash Drive Backing Tracks Pack	$79.99
00110599	USB Flash Drive Only	$50.00

VOLUME 2
00240222	C Edition	$39.99
00240227	B♭ Edition	$39.99
00240228	E♭ Edition	$39.99
00240229	Bass Clef Edition	$39.99
00240293	C Edition 6 x 9	$35.00
00125900	B♭ Edition 6 x 9	$35.00
00451088	C Edition on CD-ROM	$30.99
00125900	The Real Book – Mini Edition	$35.00
00204126	Backing Tracks on USB Flash Drive	$50.00
00204131	C Edition – USB Flash Drive Pack	$79.99

VOLUME 3
00240233	C Edition	$39.99
00240284	B♭ Edition	$39.99
00240285	E♭ Edition	$39.99
00240286	Bass Clef Edition	$39.99
00240338	C Edition 6 x 9	$35.00
00451089	C Edition on CD-ROM	$29.99

VOLUME 4
00240296	C Edition	$39.99
00103348	B♭ Edition	$39.99
00103349	E♭ Edition	$39.99
00103350	Bass Clef Edition	$39.99

VOLUME 5
00240349	C Edition	$39.99
00175278	B♭ Edition	$39.99
00175279	E♭ Edition	$39.99

VOLUME 6
00240534	C Edition	$39.99
00223637	E♭ Edition	$39.99

Also available:
00154230	The Real Bebop Book	$34.99
00240264	The Real Blues Book	$34.99
00310910	The Real Bluegrass Book	$35.00
00240223	The Real Broadway Book	$35.00
00240440	The Trane Book	$22.99
00125426	The Real Country Book	$39.99
00269721	The Real Miles Davis Book C Edition	$24.99
00269723	The Real Miles Davis Book B♭ Edition	$24.99
00240355	The Real Dixieland Book C Edition	$32.50
00294853	The Real Dixieland Book E♭ Edition	$35.00
00122335	The Real Dixieland Book B♭ Edition	$35.00
00240235	The Duke Ellington Real Book	$22.99
00240268	The Real Jazz Solos Book	$30.00
00240348	The Real Latin Book C Edition	$37.50
00127107	The Real Latin Book B♭ Edition	$35.00
00120809	The Pat Metheny Real Book C Edition	$27.50
00252119	The Pat Metheny Real Book B♭ Edition	$24.99
00240358	The Charlie Parker Real Book C Edition	$19.99
00275997	The Charlie Parker Real Book E♭ Edition	$19.99
00118324	The Real Pop Book – Vol. 1	$35.00
00240331	The Bud Powell Real Book	$19.99
00240437	The Real R&B Book C Edition	$39.99
00276590	The Real R&B Book B♭ Edition	$39.99
00240313	The Real Rock Book	$35.00
00240323	The Real Rock Book – Vol. 2	$35.00
00240359	The Real Tab Book	$32.50
00240317	The Real Worship Book	$29.99

THE REAL CHRISTMAS BOOK
00240306	C Edition	$32.50
00240345	B♭ Edition	$32.50
00240346	E♭ Edition	$35.00
00240347	Bass Clef Edition	$32.50
00240431	A-G CD Backing Tracks	$24.99
00240432	H-M CD Backing Tracks	$24.99
00240433	N-Y CD Backing Tracks	$24.99

THE REAL VOCAL BOOK
00240230	Volume 1 High Voice	$35.00
00240307	Volume 1 Low Voice	$35.00
00240231	Volume 2 High Voice	$35.00
00240308	Volume 2 Low Voice	$35.00
00240391	Volume 3 High Voice	$35.00
00240392	Volume 3 Low Voice	$35.00
00118318	Volume 4 High Voice	$35.00
00118319	Volume 4 Low Voice	$35.00

Complete song lists online at www.halleonard.com

HAL•LEONARD INSTRUMENTAL PLAY-ALONG

Your favorite songs are arranged just for solo instrumentalists with this outstanding series. Each book includes great full-accompaniment play-along audio so you can sound just like a pro!

Check out **halleonard.com** for songlists and more titles!

12 Pop Hits
12 songs
00261790	Flute	00261795	Horn
00261791	Clarinet	00261796	Trombone
00261792	Alto Sax	00261797	Violin
00261793	Tenor Sax	00261798	Viola
00261794	Trumpet	00261799	Cello

The Very Best of Bach
15 selections
00225371	Flute	00225376	Horn
00225372	Clarinet	00225377	Trombone
00225373	Alto Sax	00225378	Violin
00225374	Tenor Sax	00225379	Viola
00225375	Trumpet	00225380	Cello

The Beatles
15 songs
00225330	Flute	00225335	Horn
00225331	Clarinet	00225336	Trombone
00225332	Alto Sax	00225337	Violin
00225333	Tenor Sax	00225338	Viola
00225334	Trumpet	00225339	Cello

Chart Hits
12 songs
00146207	Flute	00146212	Horn
00146208	Clarinet	00146213	Trombone
00146209	Alto Sax	00146214	Violin
00146210	Tenor Sax	00146211	Trumpet
00146216	Cello		

Christmas Songs
12 songs
00146855	Flute	00146863	Horn
00146858	Clarinet	00146864	Trombone
00146859	Alto Sax	00146866	Violin
00146860	Tenor Sax	00146867	Viola
00146862	Trumpet	00146868	Cello

Contemporary Broadway
15 songs
00298704	Flute	00298709	Horn
00298705	Clarinet	00298710	Trombone
00298706	Alto Sax	00298711	Violin
00298707	Tenor Sax	00298712	Viola
00298708	Trumpet	00298713	Cello

Disney Movie Hits
12 songs
00841420	Flute	00841424	Horn
00841687	Oboe	00841425	Trombone
00841421	Clarinet	00841426	Violin
00841422	Alto Sax	00841427	Viola
00841686	Tenor Sax	00841428	Cello
00841423	Trumpet		

Disney Solos
12 songs
00841404	Flute	00841506	Oboe
00841406	Alto Sax	00841409	Trumpet
00841407	Horn	00841410	Violin
00841411	Viola	00841412	Cello
00841405	Clarinet/Tenor Sax		
00841408	Trombone/Baritone		
00841553	Mallet Percussion		

Dixieland Favorites
15 songs
00268756	Flute	0068759	Trumpet
00268757	Clarinet	00268760	Trombone
00268758	Alto Sax		

Billie Eilish
9 songs
00345648	Flute	00345653	Horn
00345649	Clarinet	00345654	Trombone
00345650	Alto Sax	00345655	Violin
00345651	Tenor Sax	00345656	Viola
00345652	Trumpet	00345657	Cello

Favorite Movie Themes
13 songs
00841166	Flute	00841168	Trumpet
00841167	Clarinet	00841170	Trombone
00841169	Alto Sax	00841296	Violin

Gospel Hymns
15 songs
00194648	Flute	00194654	Trombone
00194649	Clarinet	00194655	Violin
00194650	Alto Sax	00194656	Viola
00194651	Tenor Sax	00194657	Cello
00194652	Trumpet		

Great Classical Themes
15 songs
00292727	Flute	00292733	Horn
00292728	Clarinet	00292735	Trombone
00292729	Alto Sax	00292736	Violin
00292730	Tenor Sax	00292737	Viola
00292732	Trumpet	00292738	Cello

The Greatest Showman
8 songs
00277389	Flute	00277394	Horn
00277390	Clarinet	00277395	Trombone
00277391	Alto Sax	00277396	Violin
00277392	Tenor Sax	00277397	Viola
00277393	Trumpet	00277398	Cello

Irish Favorites
31 songs
00842489	Flute	00842495	Trombone
00842490	Clarinet	00842496	Violin
00842491	Alto Sax	00842497	Viola
00842493	Trumpet	00842498	Cello
00842494	Horn		

Michael Jackson
11 songs
00119495	Flute	00119499	Trumpet
00119496	Clarinet	00119501	Trombone
00119497	Alto Sax	00119503	Violin
00119498	Tenor Sax	00119502	Accomp.

Jazz & Blues
14 songs
00841438	Flute	00841441	Trumpet
00841439	Clarinet	00841443	Trombone
00841440	Alto Sax	00841444	Violin
00841442	Tenor Sax		

Jazz Classics
12 songs
00151812	Flute	00151816	Trumpet
00151813	Clarinet	00151818	Trombone
00151814	Alto Sax	00151819	Violin
00151815	Tenor Sax	00151821	Cello

Les Misérables
13 songs
00842292	Flute	00842297	Horn
00842293	Clarinet	00842298	Trombone
00842294	Alto Sax	00842299	Violin
00842295	Tenor Sax	00842300	Viola
00842296	Trumpet	00842301	Cello

Metallica
12 songs
02501327	Flute	02502454	Horn
02501339	Clarinet	02501329	Trombone
02501332	Alto Sax	02501334	Violin
02501333	Tenor Sax	02501335	Viola
02501330	Trumpet	02501338	Cello

Motown Classics
15 songs
00842572	Flute	00842576	Trumpet
00842573	Clarinet	00842578	Trombone
00842574	Alto Sax	00842579	Violin
00842575	Tenor Sax		

Pirates of the Caribbean
16 songs
00842183	Flute	00842188	Horn
00842184	Clarinet	00842189	Trombone
00842185	Alto Sax	00842190	Violin
00842186	Tenor Sax	00842191	Viola
00842187	Trumpet	00842192	Cello

Queen
17 songs
00285402	Flute	00285407	Horn
00285403	Clarinet	00285408	Trombone
00285404	Alto Sax	00285409	Violin
00285405	Tenor Sax	00285410	Viola
00285406	Trumpet	00285411	Cello

Simple Songs
14 songs
00249081	Flute	00249087	Horn
00249093	Oboe	00249089	Trombone
00249082	Clarinet	00249090	Violin
00249083	Alto Sax	00249091	Viola
00249084	Tenor Sax	00249092	Cello
00249086	Trumpet	00249094	Mallets

Superhero Themes
14 songs
00363195	Flute	00363200	Horn
00363196	Clarinet	00363201	Trombone
00363197	Alto Sax	00363202	Violin
00363198	Tenor Sax	00363203	Viola
00363199	Trumpet	00363204	Cello

Star Wars
16 songs
00350900	Flute	00350907	Horn
00350913	Oboe	00350908	Trombone
00350903	Clarinet	00350909	Violin
00350904	Alto Sax	00350910	Viola
00350905	Tenor Sax	00350911	Cello
00350906	Trumpet	00350914	Mallet

Taylor Swift
15 songs
00842532	Flute	00842537	Horn
00842533	Clarinet	00842538	Trombone
00842534	Alto Sax	00842539	Violin
00842535	Tenor Sax	00842540	Viola
00842536	Trumpet	00842541	Cello

Video Game Music
13 songs
00283877	Flute	00283883	Horn
00283878	Clarinet	00283884	Trombone
00283879	Alto Sax	00283885	Violin
00283880	Tenor Sax	00283886	Viola
00283882	Trumpet	00283887	Cello

Wicked
13 songs
00842236	Flute	00842241	Horn
00842237	Clarinet	00842242	Trombone
00842238	Alto Sax	00842243	Violin
00842239	Tenor Sax	00842244	Viola
00842240	Trumpet	00842245	Cello

Prices, contents, and availability subject to change without notice.

Disney characters and artwork ™ & © 2021 Disney

HAL•LEONARD®